INFANTRY

SWORD EXERCISE.

REVISED EDITION

ADJUTANT-GENERAL'S OFFICE, HORSE GUARDS,

JANUARY, 1845.

Published by Authority,

The Naval & Military Press Ltd

Published by the
The Naval & Military Press
in association with the Royal Armouries

Unit 10 Ridgewood Industrial Park,
Uckfield, East Sussex, TN22 5QE
Tel: +44 (0) 1825 749494
Fax: +44 (0) 1825 765701

MILITARY HISTORY AT YOUR FINGERTIPS
www.naval-military-press.com

ONLINE GENEALOGY RESEARCH
www.military-genealogy.com

ONLINE MILITARY CARTOGRAPHY
www.militarymaproom.com

ROYAL
ARMOURIES

The Library & Archives Department at the
Royal Armouries Museum, Leeds, specialises
in the history and development of armour
and weapons from earliest times to the
present day. Material relating to the
development of artillery and modern
fortifications is held at the Royal
Armouries Museum, Fort Nelson.

For further information contact:
Royal Armouries Museum, Library, Armouries Drive,
Leeds, West Yorkshire LS10 1LT
Royal Armouries, Library, Fort Nelson, Down End Road, Fareham PO17 6AN

Or visit the Museum's website at
www.armouries.org.uk

*In reprinting in facsimile from the original, any imperfections are inevitably reproduced
and the quality may fall short of modern type and cartographic standards.*

GENERAL ORDER.

HORSE GUARDS,
23rd April, 1842.

THE following *revised* Rules and Regulations for the Sword Exercise of the Infantry having been approved by the General Commanding-in-Chief, are to be observed and Practised by the several Regiments and Depôts ; and Lord Hill expects, that the General Officers charged with the Periodical Inspection of the Troops will take care to satisfy themselves, at all such Inspections, that the Instructions under this head are properly inculcated; and that both Officers and Serjeants pay due attention thereto.

The Superintendent of Sword Exercise will report to the Adjutant-General, for the information of the General Commanding-in-Chief, any case, or cases, in which these Instructions have not been carried into effect.

By Command of the Right Honourable
General Lord Hill, Commanding-in-Chief,

JOHN MACDONALD,
Adjutant-General.

CONTENTS.

———

INFANTRY SWORD EXERCISE.

Introductory Remarks.

THE following Instructions are laid down as the surest and quickest mode of forming Swordsmen; and the Drill Officers are to understand clearly, that when Recruits have completed their Preparatory and Drill Practices, *without* and *with* the sword, they need no longer be required to remember the precise order in which they are here given; nor to repeat them, if sufficiently instructed to go through the Review Exercise effectively, where every Cut, Point, and Parry is shown; and the Swordsman ought to be made so perfect in each, as to be able to give any one separately, or such of them combined, as the Drill Officer may require.

Section I.

EXTENSION MOTIONS AND POSITIONS.

The motions tend to expand the chest, raise the head, throw back the shoulders, and strengthen the muscles of the back.

The Squad being at " Attention," the caution is given :

First Extension Motions.

One—Bring the hands, arms, and shoulders to the front, the fingers lightly touching at the points, and the nails downwards ; then raise them in a circular direction well above the head, the ends of the fingers still touching, the thumbs pointing to the rear, the elbows pressed back, and the shoulders kept down.

Two—Separate and extend the arms and fingers upwards, forcing them obliquely back, until they come extended on a line with the shoulders ; and as they fall gradually from thence to the original position of " Attention," endeavour, as much as possible, to elevate the neck and chest.

Three—Turn the palms of the hands to the front, and press back the thumbs with the arms extended, and raise them to the rear until they meet above the head ; the fingers pointing upwards, and the thumbs locked with the left in front.

Four—Keep the arms and knees straight, and bend over until the hands touch the feet, the head being brought down in the same direction, and resume the " Third Motion" by raising the arms to the front.

Five—Resume the position of " Attention," as directed in " Second Motion."

The whole of these motions should be done slowly, so as to feel the exertion of the muscles throughout : and the " First" and " Second" occasionally practised with the head turned, as much as possible, to the right or left : all the motions may be performed also without any pause or separate word of command, so as to make them lead into each other, and occasionally varying them.

First Position in Three Motions.

One—Move the hands smartly to the rear, the left grasping the right arm just above the elbow, and the right supporting the left arm under the elbow.

Two—Half face to the left, turning on the heels, so that the back of the left touches the inside of the right heel, the head retaining its position to the front.

Three—Bring the right heel before the left, the feet at right angles, the right foot pointing to the front, and the weight of the body resting on the left leg.

Second Position in Two Motions.

One—Bend the knees gradually, keeping them as much apart as possible, without raising the heels, or changing the erect position of the body.

Two—Step out smartly with the right foot about eighteen inches, in line with the left heel, the weight of the body remaining on the left leg, the right knee easy and flexible.

Balance Motions.

One—Move the right foot about eight inches to the rear of the left heel, the toe lightly touching the ground, with the heel perpendicular to it, keeping the knees well apart.

Two—Raise the body gradually by the extension of the left leg.

Three—Bend the left knee, resuming the position made previous to the " Second Motion."

Four—Advance the right leg, with a smart beat of the foot, resuming the " Second Position," from which the " Balance Motions" commenced.

First Position—Extending both knees, bring the right heel up to the left.

Third Position in Two Motions.

One—Incline the right side to the front, so that the shoulder and knee are perpendicular to the point of the foot, keeping the body erect.

Two—Step out smartly to the front, about thirty-six inches, the knee perpendicular to the instep; the left knee and foot kept straight and firm, the heels in a line, the body upright, and the shoulders square to the left.

Second Extension Motions.

One—Bring the arms to the front of the body, with the hands closed and the knuckles uppermost, touching each other below the lower button of the jacket; raise them gradually until the wrists, by bearing inwards, touch the breast, the elbows being kept up; then, by forcing back the shoulders, the hands will be drawn apart, and the motion is completed by sinking the elbows, and smartly extending the arms and fingers in a diagonal line, with the right wrist as high as the head, the shoulders kept down, and the thumbs inclined to the right.

For beginners this motion may be divided by giving the word *Prepare* for the first part, and remaining perfectly steady when the hands are brought to the breast, ready to separate; then give the word *One* for the motion to be completed.

Two—Raise the body by extending the right leg.

Three—Bend the right knee, and advance the body so as to resume the " First Motion."

First Position—Spring up with the arms to the rear, and the right heel close to the left, which forms the " First Position," as before described.

Front—Come smartly to the position of " Attention;" bringing the hands and feet, in one motion, to their proper places.

In the foregoing Instructions, the Positions and Movements, preparatory to using the sword have been explained, giving a separate word of command for each motion respectively. The same positions must now be gone through

naming only (in the word of command) the position required, in order to practise the Recruit in changing the
positions readily, without losing his balance, and in quick
time,—distinguishing them by the words of command,
First, Second, and *Third.*

Positions.

First—Raising the arms to the rear, and the right
heel to the front, come at once to the " First Position."

Second—Come to " Second Position."

First	,,	" First Position."
Third	,,	" Third Position."
First	,,	" First Position."
Second	,,	" Second Position."
Third	,,	" Third Position."
Second	,,	" Second Position."

Single Attack—Raise the right foot, and beat it
smartly on the ground.

Double Attack—Raise the right foot as before, and
beat it twice on the ground—first with the heel, then
with the flat of the foot.

Advance—Move forward the right foot about six
inches, and place it smartly on the ground ; then bring
up the left lightly about the same distance.

Single Attack—As before.

Retire—Move the left foot lightly to the rear about
six inches, the weight and balance of the body being, and
continuing to rest, upon it ; then move the right foot back
the same distance, and place it smartly upon the ground.

Double Attack—As before.

Front—Resume the position of " Attention."

The object of the preceding portion of the Drill, as Positions and Movements preparatory to using the sword, is to give a free and active use of the limbs; a thorough command of which, with the knowledge of the best mode of applying the force of the muscular powers, will facilitate and give great advantage in the use of the sword, and insure a proper efficacy to the Cuts and Guards; enabling the beginner to gain more easily that pliability of strength in his position which is required either for attack or defence.

The Instructor should prove the firmness of the positions by bearing equally and firmly upon the shoulders of the Recruit in each position, and during the changes in forming the "Second Position" and "Balance Motions;" also when in the "First" of the "Second Extension Motions;" by taking hold of the right wrist with both hands, and bearing upon it in the direction of the left leg, upon the line of which the right arm should be if properly placed; and making him also in each position move the toe up and down, without its motion affecting the body, which must generally be balanced, and rest upon the left leg, thereby giving greater flexibility to the right leg in moving forward to gain distance upon an adversary—or in retiring from his reach. No precise length can be assigned in moving the right leg to the front in the "Third Position," as it depends upon the length and stride of the person; but it should not be beyond what may allow of his returning to the "First" or "Second Position" with quickness and perfect facility to himself.

When this section is practised as a drill for the limbs only, it should be performed with the left shoulder and left foot to the front, as well as with the right.

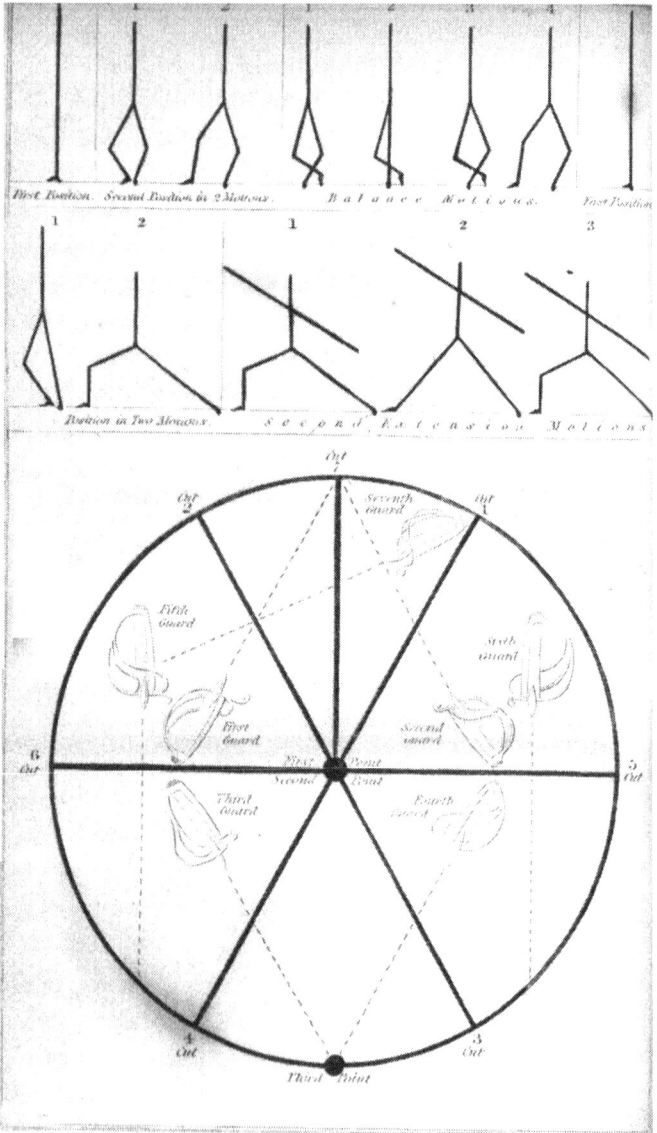

First Position. Second Position in 2 Motions. *Balance Motions.* First Position

1 2 1 2 3

Position in Two Motions. Second Extension Motions.

Out

Out
2

Seventh
Guard

Out
1

Fifth
Guard

Sixth
Guard

First
Guard

Second
Guard

6
Out

First Point
Second Point

5
Out

Third
Guard

Fourth
Guard

Out

3
Out

Third Point

MODEL OF THE TARGET

to be used in the Places of Exercise.

The Sectional Lines of Figures shew the Preparatory

Section II.

PREPARATORY INSTRUCTION WITH THE SWORD.

Explanation and Use of the Target.

THE following instructions with the Sword accord with the Target, which is to be placed so as to have its centre the height of a man's breast; from below this centre a line is drawn on the ground directly to the front, and at the distance of about ten feet the Recruit should be placed in the position of " Attention," with his left heel on the line, so that when he turns to the " First Position," his right foot may cover it.

The circular figure shows the seven " Cuts" and " Guards." The " Cuts" are directed through the centre, distinguished by lines, and named according to that number from which each cut commences.

The " Guards" are formed by holding the sword opposite to, and in the inclination of, the dotted lines which have sword-hilts attached to them; and supposing the circular figure to be about the height of a man's body, the " Cuts" and " Guards" will be regulated according to the lines described upon the circle; nor should the Recruit be practised in any other mode, until he has gained the proper direction of the " Cuts," as well as the inclination of the blade, and position of the wrist, in forming the " Guards."

The " Points" or thrusts should be directed as marked in the Target, with the wrist towards No. 1, and the edge of the sword upwards to the right, in the " First Point;" towards No. 2, with the edge upwards to the left, in the " Second Point;" and in the " Third Point," with the wrist rising to the centre, the edge upwards to the right, and the point directed as marked on the bottom of the circle.

The sectional lines of the figures over the Target represent the " Preparatory Positions."

The Target is also a guide for the Instructors in regard to the elevation of the " Cuts," " Guards," and " Parry," for the Review Exercise, as the Recruit must be made to understand clearly that the Target merely directs him *how* to *form* the "Cuts," &c., not exactly *where to cut*, as that will depend upon how the parties act when attacking each other,—as the Cuts 1, 3, and 5 can be directed at any part from head to foot on the left; and the Cuts, 2, 4, and 6, equally so on the right, the former being termed *inside*, and the latter *outside*, Cuts. The "First," "Third," and "Fifth," are the corresponding *Inside* Guards; and the "Second," "Fourth," and "Sixth," are the *Outside* Guards. When the object of being placed before the Target is well impressed upon the mind of the Recruit, he need no longer be practised in front of it, but the Instructor should consider it as a sure guide or reference for correctly forming the Guards, and giving a proper direction of the edge in making the Cuts.

In order to admit of several Recruits being exercised at the same time, circles, with the interior lines, as shown in the accompanying plate of the Target, should be delineated in the places of exercise, their centres being about four feet from the ground, and fourteen inches in diameter.

Cuts—Guards—Points—Parry.

(On Foot, and in Front of the Target.)

The Recruit being perfectly instructed in the preparatory movements, may now take the sword, making him perfectly acquainted with the strong and weak parts of it; the "Fort" (strong) being the half of the blade near the hilt, the "Feeble" (weak) the half towards the point; indeed, a knowledge of these distinctions is very material either in giving or guarding a Cut, as much depends upon their proper application. From the hilt upwards, in opposing the blade of an adversary, the strength of the defence decreases in proportion as the Cut is received towards the point; and, *vice versâ*, it increases from the point downwards. The "Fort" ought always to gain the "Feeble" of the opponent's weapon, and the Cuts should be given within eight inches of the point, so that the sword may clear itself. In delivering a Cut, it is advantageous if the "Fort" meets the adversary's "Feeble," as it will of course force his guard.

Draw Swords—Take hold of the scabbard of the sword with the left hand just below the hilt, which should be raised as high as the hip; then bring the right hand smartly across the body, grasping the hilt and turning it at the same time to the rear; raise the hand the height of the elbow, the arm being close to the body. By a second motion, draw the sword from the scabbard with an extended arm, the edge being to the rear, and lower the hand until the hilt is just below the chin, the blade perpendicular, the edge to the left, with the thumb extended on the side of the handle, and elbow close to the body, which forms the position of " Recover Swords." By a third motion, lower the wrist below, and in line with, the right hip, the elbow being drawn back, and the arm extended as much as it can be with ease, the hand slightly grasping the sword, but ready by the contraction of the fingers to resume a firm hold. The upper part of the sword will then be in the hollow of the right shoulder, with the edge to the front, which brings it to the position of " Carry Swords ;" the left hand resumes the position of " Attention," directly the sword is drawn. It is good drill practice to give the words " Two" and " Three" for the second and third motions in drawing and returning swords.

Slope Swords—Move the hand to the front in line with the elbow, which is brought close to the body, with the sword resting upon the shoulder, and edge to the front.

Return Swords—Carry the hilt to the hollow of the left shoulder (the left hand as before, raising the scabbard), with the blade perpendicular, and the back of the hand to the front: then by a quick turn of the wrist, drop the point into the scabbard, turning the edge to the rear, until the hand and elbow are in a line with each other square across the body. By a second motion, replace the sword in the scabbard, keeping the hand upon the hilt. By a third motion the hands are brought back to the position of " Attention."

Draw Swords—As before.

Slope Swords—As before.

Stand at Ease—When at close Order, the sword remains at the Slope; at Extended Order, the hands are brought together, the left supporting the right, the back of the sword resting upon the inside of the left arm, and in both the right foot moved back, with the left knee bent as usual.

Attention—Come to the position of " Slope Swords."

Prepare for Sword Exercise—Turn the body and feet to the " First Position," with the left hand resting upon the hip, and thumb to the rear.

Right Prove Distance—" Recover Swords," with the fore-finger and thumb stretched along the handle, the thumb being upon the back, with the end of the hilt in the palm of the hand. By a second motion, extend the arm to the right, and lower the sword in a horizontal direction from the shoulder, with the edge to the rear, and left shoulder square to the front.

In this, and throughout the Instructions, where a second motion is required, the word *Two* must be given, unless the practice is carried on by a Flugelman.

Slope Swords—As before.

Front Prove Distance—Raise the sword, as before, then by a second motion, step out to the "Third Position," and extend the arm, lowering the point of the sword towards the centre of the target, with the edge to the right.

Slope Swords—As before.

Assault—Raise the arm to the front, with the wrist opposite No. 1, the elbow rather bent towards the centre of the Circular Figure, and the back of the sword, near the point, resting on the shoulder, with the edge inclined to the right.

One—Extending the arm, direct the Cut to the front in a diagonal line from right to left as shown from No. 1 to No. 4; and, as the point clears the circle, turn the knuckles upwards, and continue the sweep of the sword so as to bring the point to the rear of the left shoulder, upon which it rests with the edge inclined to the left, and the wrist opposite No. 2.

Two—Direct the Cut from No. 2 to No. 3, and turn the wrist so that the sword continues its motion until the point is below the right hip, the edge downwards, the elbow bent inwards, and wrist towards No. 2.

Three—Cut diagonally upwards from No. 3 to No. 2, and continue the motion of the wrist until the point of the sword is below the left hip, the edge downwards, the elbow bent, and raised with the wrist towards No. 1.

Four—Cut diagonally upwards from No. 4 to No. 1, and turn the knuckles downwards, with the edge of the sword to the right, and the point to the rear over the right shoulder, the elbow bent, and the wrist towards No. 5.

Five—Cut horizontally from No. 5 to No. 6, and turn the knuckles up, with the edge of the sword to the left, and the point to the rear, over the left shoulder, the elbow bent, and the wrist towards No. 6.

Six—Cut horizontally from No. 6 to No. 5, and bring the hand in the direction of No. 7, the sword being on the same line over the head, with the point lowered to the rear, and the edge uppermost.

Seven—Cut vertically downwards from No. 7 to the centre of the circle, and remain with the arm extended, placing the thumb along the back of the handle, and the left shoulder pressed well back.

First Point—Turn the edge of the sword upwards to the right, and draw the wrist just above, and in front of, the right eye, the elbow well bent and raised, the left shoulder brought a little forward, and the chest drawn in. By a second motion, extend the arm and deliver the point smartly to the front, in the direction of the centre of the Target, with the wrist raised inclining to No. 1, and press back the left shoulder, so as to advance the right, which should be equally attended to in the following " Second" and " Third" Points also.

Second Point—Turn the edge upwards to the left, and draw in the elbow close to the body, with the wrist in the line above it, as high as, and in front of, the breast, the thumb being on the right of the handle. By a second motion, deliver the point, as before directed, the wrist raised inclining towards No. 2, and the edge raised with the knuckles downwards.

Third Point—Draw in the arm until the wrist touches the upper part of the hip, the thumb on the left of the handle, the edge raised to the right, the left shoulder advanced, and the hips well thrown back. By a second motion, deliver the point in the direction as marked in the Target, and raise the wrist towards the centre.

Defend—Form the "First Guard" by turning the edge to the left, the thumb resuming its grasp of the handle, and draw in the elbow close to the body; the wrist being kept to the front, and the sword placed opposite the dotted diagonal line, as shown in the Target, from the hilt marked "First Guard." In this and the following "Guards," distinguished as "Second," "Third," &c., the point should be advanced rather to the front, the left shoulder being well kept back in the Guards to the left, but rather brought forward in forming those to the right, as also in the "Seventh Guard," and "Parry."

Second—Turn the wrist with the knuckles uppermost, and the edge of the sword to the right, the sword being placed opposite the diagonal line, &c., marked "Second Guard."

Third—Turn the wrist and edge to the left, nearly as high as the shoulder, with the point lowered to the right, the sword placed, &c., as marked "Third Guard."

Fourth—Raise the elbow, as high as the shoulder, and turn the wrist and edge to the right with point to the left, the sword, &c., as marked "Fourth Guard."

Fifth—Turn the edge to the left, with the wrist as high as the shoulder, to the front and left of the body, the sword being placed opposite the perpendicular line from the hilt marked "Fifth Guard."

Sixth—Bend the wrist and turn the edge to the right so as to bring the sword opposite the perpendicular line, &c., marked "Sixth Guard."

Seventh—Raise the wrist above, and in advance of, the right ear, the elbow up, and well kept back, and the sword directed, &c., as marked "Seventh Guard."

Parry—Lower the wrist nearly close to the right shoulder, the edge to the right, the hips well pressed back, and the hilt of the sword opposite No. 1. By a second motion, turn the wrist so that the point falls towards the left rear, and forming a circle from left to right of the body, returns to its former position.

Slope Swords—As before.

The Seven Cuts and Three Points should also be practised as follows :—At the command " Assault," they are combined in regular succession, without any material pause between each, as by the proper and timely turn of the wrist the Cuts will lead into each other. They should be given strong with the edge leaning forwards, the wrist retaining its direction to the front as much as possible; and in returning to prepare for another Cut, the edge should be drawn back nearly in the same line, the arm being a little bent so as to allow a free play of the wrist, elbow, and shoulder in giving effective force to the Cut, and then extended to the utmost in the delivery of it. Whenever the Recruit fails to carry the edge well in making the assault, he should be practised in combining the cuts *One* and *Four*, repeating them several times; also *Two* and *Three* and *Five* and *Six*, taking care that the edge leads on the respective lines of the target, the wrist being darted towards the centre in each Cut.

The three Engaging Guards are now shown (the Recruit being still placed before the Target), and the " Cuts" and " Guards" combined respectively, so as to impress upon his recollections the Guard for each Cut. The Cuts and Points should be given from the wrist to the full extent of the arm, to the front, and in the "Third Position," with each cut directed no further than the centre of the circle; the Guards and Parry formed in the " First Position," in which also prepare for each point.

Guard—Advance the point of the sword, extending the arm towards the centre of the Target, with the edge downwards; then, without pause, bending the body, drawing in the chest and neck, and bringing the left shoulder a little forward, step out smartly to the "Second Position," with elbow bent and raised, so as to have the hand nearly over the right foot; the edge of the sword turned upwards, with the point lowered, and inclined to the left, the Target distinctly seen within the angle formed by the arm and sword, the hilt being inclined to No. 1, and the point directed below, and to the left of No. 4.

Inside Guard—Raise the head and body, lowering the wrist with the knuckles down, and over the foot, the point of the sword to the front, the edge to the left, and the hand as low as the elbow, a little above, and in front of, the hip, at the same time making the " Single Attack ;" the wrist is here inclined towards No. 4, the points towards No. 1.

Outside Guard—Turn the wrist with the knuckles upwards, and the edge of the sword to the right, repeating the "Single Attack," the hand inclining to No. 3, the point towards No. 2.

Cut One—Cut One and Third Position.

First Guard—First Guard and First Position.

Cut Two—Cut Two and Third Position.

Second Guard—Second Guard and First Position.

Cut Three—Cut Three and Third Position.

Third Guard—Third Guard and First Position.

Cut Four—Cut Four and Third Position.

Fourth Guard—Fourth Guard and First Position.

Cut Five—Cut Five and Third Position.

Fifth Guard—Fifth Guard and First Position.

Cut Six—Cut Six and Third Position.

Sixth Guard—Sixth Guard and First Position.

Cut Seven—Cut Seven and Third Position.

Seventh Guard—Seventh Guard and First Position.

First Point—Prepare for First Point in First Position.

Two—First Point and Third Position.

Second Point—Prepare for Second Point in First Position.

Two—Second Point and Third Position.

Third Point—Prepare for Third Point in First Position.

Two—Third Point and Third Position.

Parry—Prepare to Parry in First Position.

Two—Parry.

Guard—As before.

Slope Swords—As before.

Thus far may be considered as merely Drill Practice, and the Recruit need not be required to remember the precise order of it, after it is ascertained that he understands the object of, and can go through it correctly, and consequently is qualified to perform the " Review Exercise," as in the following Section.

Section III.

REVIEW, OR INSPECTION, EXERCISE.

THE following Exercise is similar to the latter part of the Drill Practices, and only varies by each Guard being formed after its respective Cut, without waiting for a second word of command, and after each movement of attack, springing up at once to its corresponding defensive position.

Guard—As before.

Inside Guard—As before.

Outside Guard—As before.

One—Cut " One" and " First Guard," delivering the Cut (as before directed) in the Third Position, and spring up to the First Position, in forming the Guard; and so on throughout the remaining "Cuts" and "Guards:" the same in regard to the " Points" and " Parry."

Two—Cut " Two" and " Second Guard."

Three—Cut " Three" and " Third Guard."

Four—Cut " Four" and " Fourth Guard."

Five—Cut " Five" and " Fifth Guard."

Six—Cut " Six" and " Sixth Guard."

Seven—Cut " Seven" and " Seventh Guard."

Points—Prepare for " First Point."

First—Point, and prepare for " Second Point."

Second—Point, and prepare for " Third Point."

Third—Point and prepare for " Parry."

Parry—As before.

Guard—As before.

Slope Swords—As before.

B

Although the Cuts and Guards are in the regular order from One to Seven, the Recruit should be practised to make any change of them according to the command of the Instructor, which will enable him to form more readily, and quickly, any defensive position; or to vary the movements of his attack, for which the caution "*Sword Practice*" should be given commencing with the Guard, and delivering the Inside and Outside Cuts from One to Six, but returning to Guard after each Cut, and in the same manner the "Outside Cuts" to be given from the Inside Guard, and the "Inside Cuts" from the Outside Guard. Or when any single Cut and its corresponding Guard is required, the number is to be given, and performed as in the Review Exercise; but when the Cut is to be directed for the leg—viz. Three or Four—the Caution "*For the Leg*" must be given previous to the number; and the Guard formed low accordingly:

In returning to "Guard" rise first to "Seventh Guard" and "First Position," also to the "Inside Guard" by "First Guard," and to the "Outside Guard" by "Second Guard."

Section IV.

ATTACK AND DEFENCE.

The Recruit, being now complete in giving the Cuts and forming their respective Guards must bring them into practice, according to the two following modes of exercise; the Cuts and Points being given in the Third Position; and the Guards and Parry in the First Position.

The Squads are formed in two, four, or more ranks, at the "Slope Swords," and well under the eye of the Instructor, with a distance of four paces between ranks and files; and in this formation the whole of the Drill, as shown in Sections II. and III., may be gone through, either by separate words of command, or by a Flugelman; the former being the best mode, as the swordsman is then enabled to keep his view fixed in the direction he is supposed to act.

Front Rank, Right about Face—The Files face to the Right About.

Prepare for Attack and Defence—Files oppose each other in " First Position."

Prove Distance—Files prove distance, as before directed, but remaining in " First Position."

Strict attention should be paid that the opposing Files take their proper distance, by the point of each sword touching the guard of the other, the hips being well drawn back, the front rank having their swords uppermost, and the rear rank giving way or advancing up according to the required measure; the Instructor will consequently not give the word " Slope Swords," until all remain steady at their proper distances.

Slope Swords—As before.

Guard—As before.

Inside Guard—With the "Single Attack," the Files engage on the Inside Guard, the swords joining about eight inches from the point.

Outside Guard—Change to the Outside Guard, with the " Single Attack," the swords, &c :

	Front Rank.	Rear Rank.
Left Cheek	Cut One	First Guard.
Right Cheek	Second Guard	Cut Two.
Wrist	Cut Three	Third Guard.
Leg	Fourth Guard	Cut Four.
Left Side	Cut Five	Fifth Guard.
Right Side	Sixth Guard	Cut Six.
Head	Cut Seven	Seventh Guard.
First Point	Parry and prepare for Third Point.	First Point, and prepare for Parry.
Third Point	Third Point, and prepare for Parry.	Parry, and prepare for Third Point.
Guard	As before.	
Slope Swords	As before.	

On the command for each of the above points, the defending File should spring up to the First Position, and the attacking File wait for the word " Two" to deliver it: but in the "Stick Practice" the point is to be at once given.

The movements of attack and Defence in this Practice are in the same rotation as the Review Exercise; and as they show the application of the Cuts and Guards, both (particularly the Cuts) should be made with the same precision as at the Target; nor should one sword bear upon the other, but the wrist be kept well up, and ready to renew any requisite movement. Strict attention should be observed that, after proving distance, the Files do not move their left feet, unless ordered otherwise. The Front Rank invariably commences, but equal practice should be given to both. The " Second Point" is omitted in this Practice, as the " Parry" would probably disarm the opponent.

The following Practice is intended to exercise the Drill in giving, defending, and returning the " Point" quickly, and may be continued eight or ten times, by a quick successive word of command, according to the abilities of the parties engaged ; it is also the most effectual defence against the Pike or Bayonet, except the " Fifth Guard," which, if well timed, enables you, under cover of your sword, to seize the musquet with the left hand and cut " Six" at your opponent's neck.

Point and Parry.

	Front Rank.	Rear Rank.
Guard	As before.	
Third Point	Prepare to give Third Point.	Prepare to Parry.
Point	Advance the body by extending the left leg, giving Third Point, and when parried, draw back the arm ready to "Parry"	Parry, and prepare for third Point.
Point	Draw back the body by nearly extending the right leg, Parry, &c.	Third Point, &c.
Guard	As before	
Slope Swords	As before	

Equal practice may be given to all by the caution which Rank is to commence, the Front Rank always doing so (as above mentioned), unless otherwise directed. The Squads here also should occasionally be formed Rank Entire, and put through the Guards and Points in each position, particularly in the First, and to change frequently from the "First" to the "Third," and from the "Second" to the "Third," in giving Point.

Section V.

STICK DRILL.

As no Exercise with the sword can be properly attained without some mode of loose or independent practice, Sticks should be substituted for Swords, as, in Fencing, foils are used for the acquirement of that Art; but before such practice is allowed, the following five combinations of Attack and Defence are to be well practised and executed. The Sticks are to be about forty inches long, and not so weak as to bend, the leather hilts being merely large enough to cover the hand, without confining it; and on no account are the Masks to be omitted, as they enable those who practise to cut or thrust with more confidence. The same formation is continued as for the " Attack and Defence ;" also the proving distance; and the two First Practices are to be the same as previously gone through with Swords in Sect. IV. In the Third Practice, the Cuts at the leg are given with the Third Position ; those at the head and neck in the First, but with caution and lightly, as both Cuts being given at the same time, the File, giving the Cut at the leg, has not the power of defending himself; thus showing the advantage of shifting the leg, when engaged at the proper distance. In the Fourth and Fifth Practices, the Attack is made as usual with the Third, and the Defence, in the First, Position.

First Practice.

Guard—Continuing the same words of command and movements as in the " Attack and Defence" in Section IV.

Second Practice.

Guard—Continuing, &c., as the " Point and Parry."

Third Practice.

	Front Rank.	Rear Rank.
Guard	As before.	
Leg	Cut Four at Leg	Cut Seven at Head.
Inside Guard	As before.	
Leg	Cut Six at Leg	Cut Six at Neck.
Outside Guard	As before.	
Leg	Cut Five at Leg	Cut Five at Neck.
Guard	As before.	
Slope Swords	As before.	

Fourth Practice.

Guard	As before.	
Head	Cut Seven	Seventh Guard.
Head	Seventh Guard	Cut Seven.
Leg	Cut Four	Seventh Guard.
Leg	Seventh Guard	Cut Four.
Head	Cut Seven	Seventh Guard.
Head	Seventh Guard	Cut Seven.
Guard	As before.	
Slope Swords	As before.	

Fifth Practice.

Guard	As before.	
Head	Cut Seven	Seventh Guard.
Head	Seventh Guard	Cut Seven.
Arm	Cut Two	Second Guard.
Head	Seventh Guard	Cut Seven.
Head	Cut Seven	Seventh Guard.
Arm	Second Guard	Cut Two.
Head	Cut Seven	Seventh Guard.
Head	Seventh Guard	Cut Seven.
Right Side	Cut Six	Sixth Guard.
Head	Seventh Guard	Cut Seven.
Head	Cut Seven	Seventh Guard.
Right Side	Sixth Guard	Cut Six.
Guard	As before.	
Slope Swords	As before.	

Particular attention should be paid, that in the Attack the wrist preserves, as much as possible, the line of the direction in which the Cut is given; and, in each position of defence, that it only deviates from it sufficiently to form the Guard: taking care to have the wrist, elbow, and shoulder supple and easy, so as to be ready to deliver a Cut, Thrust, or perform any other movement of Attack or Defence.

It is good practice in the Drill with Sticks, for each movement of Attack and Defence to be first performed in two motions, by the Sticks slightly touching the part to which it is directed, and the defence only formed at the word "Two:" this enables the Instructor to see that the Attacking Files give their Cuts and Thrusts fully home, and according to rule: and that the files on the defensive come to a firm and correct position; it also greatly assists in judging exactly where the weapons should cross each other.

As in the preceding Section, the whole should be reversed by the Rear Rank commencing instead of the Front; and, when perfect by word of command, in all the practices, they are to be performed in quick time, the Instructor naming only the Practice required, previously giving the caution, "*Stick Drill by Practice Divisions.*"

The Point being generally the most effective, should occasionally be substituted for the Cut, when an opportunity offers of giving it, either in the attack, or in a quick return from a defensive Guard,—the "First Point" being more speedily given from the Second, Fifth, and Seventh Guards; the "Second Point" from the First and Third Guards; the "Third Point" from the Fourth and Sixth Guards; and the Point, so given may be defended by the same Guard as against the Cut, the Thrust being delivered by an immediate extension of the arm at the moment the point is in the proper line of direction.

A Feint is a Half cut, or Thrust, menacing an attack at one part, whilst the intention is to direct it at another; and the true Cut, or Thrust, should be given as the opponent answers to the Feint.

When perfectly exercised and complete in the above Drill, the Independent Practice may be tried (under proper control) by the Files attacking each other, as in single combat with Sword, and delivering such Cuts or Thrusts as their judgment directs, but paying strict attention to the following rules as their guidance.

Rules for the Independent Practice with Sticks.

The Cuts and Thrusts must not be given too strongly, or so as to cause anger or irritation.

Each Cut or Thrust to be acknowledged on the party receiving it, by his passing the Stick into the left hand, the opponent at the same time recovering to an Engaging Guard.

The combat to be renewed out of distance, the parties coming within it cautiously, so that neither is taken by surprise.

No two Cuts or Thrusts to be made upon the same lunge, or the opponents making either at the same time ; in such case the Cut given in the Third Position to be considered effective.

No shifting from any Cut or Thrust, unless it can be effected with security.

All Cuts being made from a defensive position, great attention should be paid in immediately returning to such, as soon as the Cut or Thrust is delivered.

No practice to be allowed without masks ; and as the Stick is the substitute for the Sword, the Cut can only be considered fair and effective when given with that part which corresponds with the edge : nor should any movement of attack or defence be attempted with the Stick, which could not be performed, or would not be risked, in a combat with Swords.

Section VI.

GENERAL OBSERVATIONS and DIRECTIONS.

The exercise of the Sword consists of seven Cuts or directions of the edge ; the same number of Guards or defensive positions ; the Point (or Thrust) given with the nails up or down; and a circular motion of the blade, termed the Parry : therefore, whatever may be the attack or defence, it can only be formed by having recourse to some of the above movements, or a combination of them.

By engaging, which is generally the action of joining Swords with an opponent, previous to the attack, there should be only a slight pressure on his blade, so that the hand or wrist may be more susceptible of any motion ; and although the Guard, as also the Inside or Outside Guard, affords protection at the moment, they are merely considered as preparatory to any offensive or defensive movements, varying the latter according to the points liable to be attacked.

In all attacks, whether Cuts or Thrusts, the motion ought to increase in velocity, the greatest force being given at the last : the same rule should be observed in stepping out to the *Second* and *Third* Positions; but in recovering, the reverse is to be attended to, as the first part is the quickest ; and nothing is of more importance than that the eye should follow that of the opponent, still watching the movement of the wrist, and slightly glancing at the part where you intend to Cut or Thrust ; taking care never to look at your own Sword, which will invariably follow the eye wherever you direct it.

Although each Cut has its Guard, according to the number, yet it does not follow that the File on the defensive is always to have recourse to it, as he may frequently be enabled to secure himself more effectually and quicker, by forming some other Guard ; if, for example, he makes the Cut *Six* at the body, and his opponent, after defending by the *Sixth Guard*, return the Cut *One* at the breast, then the *Fifth Guard* becomes the quickest movement of defence ; but if the opponent has defended by the *Second Guard* previous to his return of the Cut *One*, then the *First Guard* is the quickest formed ; consequently the *First* and *Fifth Guards* each defend the Cuts *One* or *Five*, the *Second* and *Sixth Guards* each defend the Cuts *Two* or *Six* according as they may be given high or low ; and if the *Third* or *Fourth Guards* are required for the defence of the leg, the arm must be extended, so that the *Fort* of the blade may receive the *Feeble* of the opponent's weapon; bearing well in mind, however, that in all Cuts at the leg, when at the proper distance, the shifting of your own leg, and delivering a Cut at the same moment becomes the most effective and advantageous defence ; particularly to a tall man (even in every part of the body), when engaged with another of lesser stature, or length of arm, as he will be out of his opponent's reach, whilst the latter may be within his.

The Art of defence does not, in fact, so much consist in your own strength of position, as in effecting a decidedly quick movement in that direction where your opponent has the least means of resistance, especially in defending against the *Point*, when the *First, Third*, and *Fifth Guards* are the most effective against the *First* and *Third Points;* and the *Second, Fourth*, and *Sixth Guards* against the *Second Point;* provided the wrist happens to be so previously placed, that the requisite Guards may be quickly formed : and the *First Point* is more speedily given in return from the *Second, Fifth*, and *Seventh Guards;* the *Second Point* from the *First* and *Third Guards;* and the *Third Point* from the *Fourth* and *Fifth* Guards.

If opposed to the Small Sword, have recourse to the Cuts *Three* and *Four*, directing them at the arm, by which means there is every probability of the Cuts taking effect, as it must always come within range of the edge, before the point can be sufficiently advanced to reach your body : if the above Cuts are quickly given and continued, they will always be found advantageous in advancing against the Small Sword, as they constitute an attack and form a defence at the same moment ; but should the opponent be the most skilful and quickest in his movements, then it is best to retire whilst giving them, cautiously preserving the proper distance, so that each Cut may just reach the fore part of his arm.

The *Second Point*, if delivered as a first movement, should be given with great caution, the wrist being then in a position so liable to the disarm ; it should be resorted to chiefly in the return, or after a Feint from the *Outside* or *Inside Guards*; if from the former, Feint *Third Point* under, and deliver *Second Point* over, the arm; if from the latter, Feint Cut *Two*, and continue the sweep of the Sword until the point is sufficiently lowered to deliver without pause the *Second Point* at the body under the arm.

Cutting within the Sword may be resorted to, if an adversary does not form sufficient opposition in making his attack, when, by a quick turn of the wrist, on the side you defend, the Inside Cuts may be given from the Outside Guards, and the Outside Cuts from the Inside Guards. The two most effective are after the Second and Fourth Guards, viz., the Cut Five at the neck from the former, and at the leg from the latter: the Drawing Cut as according to the mode laid down; and the Thrusting Cut, by forcing the edge forward from the *Feeble* to the *Fort* of the blade, either after a weak defence of an adversary, or by his laying himself sufficiently open for you to deliver it.

The line of Direction is, in a general sense, the position of the feet, body, and arms kept invariably in a straight line on the proper position of " Guard;" it is sometimes towards the arm and point of the Sword, in Guarding, Parrying, and Thrusting: if you form your Guards too wide, you are said to deviate from the Line of Direction, and consequently leave some part of your body unguarded; if you make a Thrust at an adversary, without covering yourself and resisting his blade, you are also said to deviate from the Line of Direction; your Point, too, deviates from the line of Direction when not steadily directed at your adversary's body.

Lunge is the act of extending yourself on the Line of Direction, the full distance of your stride, in order to make your approaches to an adversary's body in delivering a Cut or Thrust.

Recovering is the act of resuming the position of Guard, after having made a lunge at your adversary; a quick and easy recovery to Guard is very essential to your own safety.

If opposed to the Bayonet or Pike, your adversary, from the length of those weapons, can keep you at a distance as to be out of your reach, whilst you are within his : you must therefore endeavour to assail his advanced wrist, or close upon him by forcing his weapon aside, by the " Parry" or " *Fourth Guard.*" The " *Fifth Guard*" is, however, more effective, as he has less power of resistance, or of clearing his weapon, which may be thrown out of his hand, or you may seize it with your left hand, which is not so easily done if it had been warded off to the right, as your defence is always more effective on the left, than on the right; but, although he wields it with both hands, you will find it easier to bear it off to the right; and he has less power of resistance, or of clearing himself, if you force it to the left; besides, you have then the additional advantage of seizing it with the left hand, which you cannot so easily do on the right.

Against a mounted opponent you should endeavour to gain his left side, where he has less power of defending himself or his horse, and cannot reach so far on attacking as on the right. In assailing the horse also, you may make him unruly, and less under command of his rider, upon which his safety very materially depends; bearing in mind the advantage you have in the power of being in, and out of, reach nearly at the same instant; whilst the motions of the horse being too slow and cumbersome for that purpose, afford the dismounted Swordsman (if he possesses proper nerve) a decided advantage over his mounted opponent.

Although a regular mode is laid down for drawing the Sword, yet occasional practice should be given to come to the *Guard* immediately, and at any required point, without going through the Parade Motions, &c., thereby preparing the Swordsman for any sudden attack of an enemy.

Many similar remarks will naturally occur to those who have practical experience; and the Instructors should endeavour as much as possible, in their directions to the Recruit, to impress them upon his mind by such occasional observations as they become most applicable. Opportunities of thus explaining may often be taken during the pauses of rest, as no Squad should be kept too long either in the Positions or Movements; and where Recruits are more deficient than the others, the whole should be made to cease for the moment, and those who have gone wrong be corrected.

Section VII.

OFFICER'S SALUTE.

The Officers to be formed in line at four paces distant from each other. " Standing at Ease" with the point of the sword lowered between the feet, the edge to the right, and left hand covering the right.

Attention—Carry Swords as before.

Rear Rank take Open Order—" Recover Swords," and move forward an oblique pace to the left, so as to be placed in front, and just clear, of the first File.

March—Advance three paces to the Front, and bring

the Sword to the " Port," the blade being diagonally
across the body, the edge upwards, and arm nearly extended; the left elbow bent with the hand as high, and
in front of the shoulder; holding the blade between the
fore-finger and thumb, the knuckles to the front, and
elbows close to the side.

Present Arms—" Recover Swords" at the second
motion of the Firelock, and at the third motion lower the
Sword (to the full extent of the arm) to the right, with
the edge to the left and point in the direction of the right
foot, the elbow close to the side, at the same time raising
the left arm as high as the shoulder, and bringing the hand
round by a circular motion over the peak of the cap, the
knuckles uppermost and fingers extended.

Shoulder Arms—" Recover Swords" at the first motion
of the Firelock, and at the second motion " Port Swords."

Rear Rank take Close Order—" Right Face," and
as the right foot is drawn to the Rear " Recover Swords."
March—Move back into the front Rank, " Front"
and " Carry Swords."
The salute on the march is to commence when at ten
paces from the Reviewing Officer, the Officer on the right
giving the signal to prepare the other Officers by raising
the fingers of the left hand two paces previous to saluting;
the Sword is then raised by extending the arm to the
right, and by a circular motion brought to the Recover;
and continuing the motion to the right shoulder, from
whence the sword is lowered, and the left hand is then
gradually raised over the peak of the cap in the manner
before directed. The time for completing the Salute is
six paces, commencing with the left foot, and may be
divided (for Drill practice) as follows:—First Pace, the
sword raised to the right; Second Pace, to the Recover;
Third Pace, to the right Shoulder; Fourth Pace, the
Sword lowered to the right; Fifth Pace, the left arm
raised; Sixth Pace, hand brought to the peak of the cap.
The above four motions with the sword, when on the
" March" must be gracefully combined into one con-
tinuous movement.

The head should be slightly turned towards the Reviewing Officer whilst passing him; and, having done so, six paces, and given the signal (as before) "Recover Swords" one pace, and "Port" in the following pace.

On the March, or when manœuvring, the Sword may be carried to the full extent of the arm, the guard of the hilt resting upon the inside of the fingers, the back of the blade being against the hollow of the shoulder.

WORDS OF COMMAND

THROUGHOUT THE

Progressive Instructions of the Drill.

Those words printed in *Italics* are to serve as a caution only.

SECTION I.

EXTENSION MOTIONS AND POSITIONS.

Attention.

First Extension Motions.
One—Two—Three—Four—Five.

First Position in Three Motions.
One—Two—Three.

Second Position in Two Motions.
One—Two.

Balance Motions.
One—Two—Three—Four.
First Position.

Third Position in Two Motions.
One—Two.

Second Extension Motions.
One—Two—Three.
First Position.
Front.
Stand at Ease.

Attention.

Positions.

First—Second—First—Third.

First—Second—Third—Second.

Single Attack—Double Attack.

Advance—Single Attack.

Retire—Double Attack.

Front—Stand at Ease.

Section II.

PREPARATORY INSTRUCTION WITH THE SWORD.

Attention.

Draw Swords—Return Swords.

Draw Swords—Slope Swords.

Stand at Ease.

Attention.

Prepare for Sword Exercise.

Right Prove Distance—Slope Swords.

Front Prove Distance—Slope Swords.

Assault.

One—Two—Three—Four—Five—Six—Seven.

First Point–Two–Second Point–Two–Third Point–Two.

Defend.

Second—Third—Fourth—Fifth—Sixth—Seventh.

Parry—Two.

Slope Swords.

Stand at Ease.

Attention.

Guard—Inside Guard—Outside Guard.

Cut One	First Guard
Cut Two	Second Guard
Cut Three	Third Guard
Cut Four	Fourth Guard
Cut Five	Fifth Guard
Cut Six	Sixth Guard
Cut Seven	Seventh Guard
First Point	Two
Second Point	Two
Third Point	Two
Parry	Two
Guard	Slope Swords

Stand at Ease.

This completes the Drill Practices, which need not be kept up, or repeated when the Recruit is able to go through the Review Exercise effectively, as shown in the following Section III.

Section III.

REVIEW, OR INSPECTION EXERCISE.

Attention.

Prepare for Sword Exercise.

Right Prove Distance—Slope Swords.
Front Prove Distance—Slope Swords.
Guard—Inside Guard—Outside Guard.
One—Two—Three—Four—Five—Six—Seven.
Points—First—Second—Third—Parry.
Guard—Slope Swords.

Sword Practice.

Guard.

Inside and Outside Cuts.

One—Two—Three—Four—Five—Six.
Inside Guard.

Outside Cuts.

Two—Four—Six.
Outside Guard.

Inside Cuts.

One—Three—Five.
Guard—Slope Swords.
Stand at Ease.

Section IV.

ATTACK AND DEFENCE.

Attention.

Front Rank, Right about Face.
Prepare for Attack and Defence.
Prove Distance—Slope Swords.
Guard—Inside Guard—Outside Guard.
Left Cheek—Right Cheek—Wrist—Leg.
Left Side—Right Side—Head.
First Point—Two—Third Point—Two.
Guard—Slope Swords.

Point and Parry.

Guard—Third Point—Point.
Point (continuing as long as requisite).
Guard—Slope Swords.
Stand at Ease.

SECTION V.

STICK DRILL.

First Practice.

Guard—Continuing the same Words of Command and Movements, as in the " Attack and Defence," in Section IV., omitting the word " Two" in the delivery of each Point.

Second Practice.

Guard—Continuing, &c. as the " Point and Parry," but not exceeding Six Points.

Third Practice.

Guard—Leg—Inside Guard—Leg.
Outside Guard—Leg—Guard.
Slope Swords.

Fourth Practice.

Guard—Head—Head—Leg.
Leg—Head—Head-Guard.
Slope Swords.

Fifth Practice.

Head—Head—Arm.
Head—Head—Arm.
Head—Head—Right Side.
Head—Head—Right Side.
Slope Swords.

When perfect by Word of Command, the whole of this Section is to be performed in Quick Time, by the Drill Officer naming only the Practice required, but first giving the caution—*Stick Drill, by Practice Divisions.*